A Nurturing Heart

VONETTE *Zachary* BRIGHT

NewLife
PUBLICATIONS

My Heart in His Hands Bible Study: A Nurturing Heart

Published by

NewLife Publications

A ministry of Campus Crusade for Christ

P.O. Box 620877

Orlando, FL 32862-0877

ISBN 1-56399-177-2

Design and production by Genesis Group

Cover by Koechel-Peterson Design

Printed in the United States of America

Unless otherwise indicated, Scripture quotations are from the *New International Version*, © 1973, 1978, 1984 by the International Bible Society. Published by Zondervan Bible Publishers, Grand Rapids, Michigan.

For more information, write:

L.I.F.E., Campus Crusade for Christ—P.O. Box 40, Flemington Markets, 2129, Australia

Campus Crusade for Christ of Canada—Box 529, Sumas, WA 98295

Campus Crusade for Christ—Fairgate House, King's Road, Tyseley, Birmingham, B11 2AA, United Kingdom

Lay Institute for Evangelism, Campus Crusade for Christ—P.O. Box 8786, Auckland, 1035, New Zealand

Campus Crusade for Christ—9 Lock Road #3-03, PacCan Centre, Singapore

Great Commission Movement of Nigeria—P.O. Box 500, Jos, Plateau State, Nigeria, West Africa

Campus Crusade for Christ International—100 Lake Hart Drive, Orlando, FL 32832, USA

Contents

My Dear Friends

I want to welcome you to this Bible study series for women! I'm excited about the opportunity to walk through the Scriptures with you as we explore all that God's Word has for the busy woman of today.

Every unique detail of a woman's life fits into a grand and glorious plan. My prayer is that women of all ages will desire to have a deeper relationship with God, and to discover the joys of knowing Him and His plan for their lives.

God's Word speaks so directly to every aspect of a woman's life. It fills us with wisdom, imparts God's love, and provides ample instructions for our daily walk. The Scriptures tell us the results we can expect when we live in agreement with God's plan, and what we can expect if we do not live as He directs.

The Bible has much to say about its value and relevance for our lives today. It gives us guidance: "Your word is a lamp to my feet and a light for my path" (Psalm 119:105). It gives understanding: "The unfolding of your words gives light; it gives understanding to the simple" (Psalm 119:130). It is not made up of cold, dead words, but living, Spirit-filled words that can affect our hearts and our lives: "For the word of God is living and active. Sharper than any double-edged sword, it penetrates even to dividing soul and spirit, joints and marrow; it judges the thoughts and attitudes of the heart" (Hebrews 4:12).

When I wrote the devotional books for the series *My Heart In His Hands*, it was with the desire to encourage women and to help them realize that God is interested and involved in the details of their lives. My goal was to provide a practical and systematic way for a woman to examine her heart and recognize how beautifully God has created her. This set of study guides has been designed to complement each seasonal devotional.

Each study guide has been developed prayerfully and can be used for individual or group study. Perhaps you are part of a group that meets regularly to study and discuss the precious treasures of God's Word. I have been a part of such groups for many years, and I am still overjoyed to meet with these women.

Whether you will study on your own or with others, it is my heartfelt prayer that you will open your heart to His Word and enjoy the blessing of resting confidently in His hands.

From my heart to yours,

Vonette Z. Bright

How to Use This Study

The *My Heart in His Hands* Bible study series is designed for the busy woman who desires a deeper walk with God. The twenty lessons in *A Nurturing Heart* embrace the glorious truth that any Christian woman can live a victorious lifestyle—no matter what life throws in her path.

A Nurturing Heart provides everything you need to understand biblical principles and use them to transform your life. Whether you are working hard at your career, involved in full-time ministry, knee-deep in preschoolers, or raising teenagers, you can find the time to complete the short lessons and receive encouragement for your day. The questions require less time than most courses so that you can fit Bible study into your hectic schedule. The refreshing look at Scripture passages will help you apply God's Word to your daily needs.

You can use this book as an individual study during your quiet time with God, or as a group study with other women. (A Discussion Guide with answers to the Bible questions is located at the back of this book to help a group facilitator.) It can also be used as a companion to the *My Heart in His Hands* devotional series.

The book contains an in-depth look at the lives of two women: a biblical portrait of a godly woman and an inspirational portrait of an outstanding contemporary woman. These portraits, woven throughout the book, give insights into a nurturing heart.

Each lesson includes these parts:

- His Word—a Scripture passage to read
- Knowing His Heart—understanding God's Word
- Knowing My Heart—personal questions to consider
- My Heart in His Hands—a timely quote to ponder

Whether to start your morning or end your day, you can use this study to focus on God's Word and on His marvelous works in your life. As you apply these principles, you will truly discover a nurturing heart!

A Nurturing Heart

Do you know someone who can grow anything? Her house-plants flourish and her spring flowerbeds soon overflow with blossoms. She is definitely the one you ask to care for your plants when you are away from home.

We can only imagine Eve's ability to tend the Garden of Eden. But we do know that God created woman with the desire and ability to nurture living things. Women are relational by God's design and, according to many studies, are generally better nurturers than men.

Nurturing, however, takes time, yet we live in an age of instant gratification. We shop on the Internet and have our purchases at our door the next morning. We fill our grocery carts with "quick," instant foods and stock up on microwave meals that take just minutes to prepare. I have actually become impatient waiting for one-hour photo processing.

You could probably add many things to this list. Creative minds have devised ways to bypass the time-consuming processes of years past to give us anything we want at breakneck speed. Much of the technology is wonderful and many of the products are great.

While organizing the linen closet, I discovered something that illustrates what we have lost in our demand for "instant" everything. Two quilts were stacked on the shelf: one was handmade by Bill's grandmother and given to Bill and me as a wedding gift; the other was machine-made and was ordered from a catalog. I bought it because it was the color and size I wanted to use as a decorator item. The quilt from Bill's grandmother, on the other hand, was a patchwork of fabric and had been created to keep the family warm on cold mid-western nights.

In my family, my grandmothers and aunties spent hours cutting and clocking fabric and preparing the various elements of a quilt. Many of the family quilts were sewn at the Ladies Missionary Circle meetings where two quilts were usually in process—one for a missionary family and one for a church family. I know God blessed the efforts of those dear women, but some of the greatest blessings came from the conversations shared around the quilting frame as the women worked with thimbled fingers and quilting needles. This is where much of the practical advice and wisdom of godly women was passed to the next generation. Shared spiritual victories encouraged younger believers to stand strong in their faith.

The nurturing process of older women teaching younger women homemaking techniques and mothering skills has largely been replaced with TV programs and magazines. Not only is much of this information unbiblical, but it is missing human interaction, the spiritual dynamic of the heart of one woman nurturing another woman.

If you carefully watch a woman tend her plants, you will see that there isn't a "secret" procedure or high-potency plant food that produces healthy and beautiful plants, but rather a consistent nurturing process. Nurturing people in the Lord also requires consistency—whether we are working with our own children, neighbors, a Sunday school class at church, or friends in the workplace. The following lessons will help you as you reach out to others with God's principles and love them through the power of His Holy Spirit.

The Heart of Jochebed

When you hear a news report that a young child has disappeared, you undoubtedly feel as I do—heartsick. I can only imagine the anguish the child's mother must feel. The thought that adults could harm children is beyond my comprehension.

Yet, history is filled with accounts of children being used as sacrifices and of harsh rulers commanding their execution. Can you imagine the fear that struck the heart of Jochebed, the mother of Moses, when she heard Pharaoh's edict that all newborn Hebrew boys were to be thrown into the Nile? Her pregnancy would bring the third child into the family of Amran. (See Numbers 26:59; Aaron was three when Moses was born, and it is believed that Miriam was around ten years of age.) Surely, until the moment of the birth, Jochebed was haunted by fears of what would happen if her child was male.

When the midwife announced the delivery of a baby boy, the joy of holding him was no doubt overshadowed by anxiety over what was to happen next—the slaughter of her baby. Jochebed saw that her newborn was "a fine child" and "no ordinary child" (Exodus 2:2; Hebrews 11:23). As she held Moses, she knew that he had been sent by God. She managed to hide the infant for a time, but when she could conceal him no longer, she used her creativity to make a waterproof basket to cradle her tiny son. (Read the story in Exodus 2.)

Jochebed must have had great faith in God's providence as she set the basket by the bank of the Nile. Every mother who has watched a young child walk away for his first day of school, or has settled a teenager in a college dorm and driven away with that sinking uncertainty, can surely understand what a woman of faith Jochebed must have been.

Soon, the Pharaoh's daughter came down to bathe in the river and spotted the basket among the reeds. As she opened the basket, the baby's helpless cries touched her heart. "This is one of the Hebrew babies," she said.

Then Miriam approached her. "Should I go and get one of the Hebrew women to nurse the baby for you?"

"Yes, go," Pharaoh's daughter replied.

So the girl rushed home and returned with Jochebed, the baby's mother.

"Take this baby and nurse him for me, and I will pay you," Pharaoh's daughter told her.

So Jochebed was able to take her baby home and nurse him —with pay! When he was older, she brought him back to Pharaoh's daughter, who adopted him as her son.

A woman's heart is designed by God to nurture. The style and form of nurturing may vary, but the basic desire to care for, protect, and guide other human beings is evident in most women. The impact of Jochebed's nurturing heart in the lives of each of her three children was evident in how they developed into godly adults (see Micah 6:4). Miriam was a gifted poetess and musician. Aaron became Israel's first high priest. Moses became one of the greatest national leaders the world has ever known.

God rewarded Jochebed's nurturing heart. She is the first person in Scripture to have a name compounded with *Jah*—or Jehovah—and she is listed as one of the faithful in Hebrews 11:23.

The Heart of Mary Lee Bright

Bearing a child in the 1920s was different than having a baby today. Then, many Americans lived in rural settings, and the average family had five or more children. Today, one or two children is the norm.

Early in the 20th century, Mary Lee Bright raised seven children. She expressed her devotion to each child through simple and thoughtful acts, such as walking down a rutted road, lantern in hand, to meet her sons and daughters when after-school activities kept them late. Her tender heart knew the fears a young child might have when walking alone in the dark.

Mrs. Bright maintained a rambling, two-story house situated on a five-thousand-acre ranch outside of Coweta in northeast Oklahoma. She was well aware of the political and social concerns of the day, but in 1921, her worries focused on the baby she was carrying. She had lost one son at childbirth, and now she was told that her life was at risk with her current pregnancy. The doctor gave her little hope that both she and the baby would make it. So she prayed, not for her own life, but that she would be able to give birth to a healthy child, and promised God that this baby would be dedicated to His service. Her baby boy was born healthy, and Mary Bright began the years of nurturing the child she had dedicated to God. Not until twenty-four years later, when Bill Bright, my husband, announced his own decision to follow Christ, would she tell him of her prayer to God regarding his life and destiny.

During Bill's childhood, her life spoke to him in many ways of her devotion to her Lord. She read from her Bible each morning and evening and sang hymns as she went about her work.

"She lived a very selfless life," Bill recalls. "Our neighbors would turn to her when they were ill, when they needed anything. She was very sensitive about literature, poetry, art, and those finer qualities. She brought that spirit into the community.

"She lived for her husband and children. She worked hard, but she always had time for us. At the end of the day—after we had all gone to bed—she stayed up reading her Bible and praying. I remember that vividly."

My mother-in-law was truly a Proverbs 31 woman. All of the 109 members of her family, from children to great-great grandchildren, have risen up to call her "blessed." They all made their way to her bedside to express their love and appreciation for her before her death at age ninety-three. Even today, this woman continues to have an influence through the lives of her children.

My husband's description of his mother gives an exquisite picture of a godly, nurturing heart. "The greatest influence in my life has been my mother's life and prayers. She was the most godly person I have ever known. She was quiet and self-effacing, but by her attitude and actions, she demonstrated a rare Christlike quality. Mother's life was characterized by commitment to Christ, a selfless spirit, a life of prayer, and a life in the Word. She sought no credit, glory, or honor. She loved Jesus with all of her heart and lived an exemplary life."

As godly women, we have the privilege of nurturing others in the same way Mary Lee Bright cared for those she loved. One of our most important roles is to care for those around us with the attitude Christ has toward His children.

PART 1

The Nurturing Instinct

The tenderest example of nurturing is a mother nursing her newborn. But nurturing doesn't end after the newborn stage. All of our lives we need nurturing, whether it comes from our parents, family, or friends.

God has given each woman a nurturing instinct to equip her for raising children. In recent decades, there has been an effort to pull women away from their mothering roles, arguing that they could find greater fulfillment in a career. But as the biological clock ticks closer to the end of child-bearing years, many women suddenly sense a need to fulfill their nurturing instinct.

Karen Hughes, White House counselor for President George W. Bush, shocked the news media by resigning her influential position and moving back to Texas to spend more time with her family. Many less-prominent women are doing the same, as they see their children growing up and becoming more independent. They realize that nurturing must take place during a certain period in a child's life, or the opportunity is lost.

The Bible also talks about spiritual nurturing, the God-given desire to help another person grow to be more like Christ.

Scripture compares a Christian's stages of spiritual growth to those of physical growth. Peter writes, "Like newborn babies, crave pure spiritual milk, so that by it you may grow up in your salvation, now that you have tasted that the Lord is good" (1 Peter 2:2,3). When a baby craves milk, she is inconsolable until she receives it.

God expects us to nurture other Christians like a mother feeds her baby. Paul explains how he nurtured the Corinthian believers: "I gave you milk, not solid food, for you were not yet ready for it" (1 Corinthians 3:2). We are to be aware of the needs of other believers and help them learn how to feed themselves on the spiritual food of God's Word.

I've been privileged to work with many young believers who desired to become more like Jesus. What a joy each relationship has been as together we enjoyed God's presence, studied His Word, and delighted in answered prayer. The fellowship between two believers who have a nurturing bond is unbelievably satisfying and wonderful.

God has equipped women with skills that we can use to spiritually nurture other believers. As we seek His guidance, the Holy Spirit will develop our spiritual nurturing instinct to enable us to serve Him by serving others. This is discipleship.

How is your spiritual nurturing instinct? What are you allowing the Holy Spirit to do through you to strengthen your walk with the Lord and to edify those around you? Our first five lessons give insight on spiritual nurturing.

By God's Design

Part of the nurturing instinct God has given us is a desire to put things in order. As women, we spend much time each day trying to arrange the things in our lives—cleaning our homes, washing and folding clothes, fixing our hair. Although these tasks need to be done, is what we're doing the most productive in God's eyes? How can we use our need for order to help others? God has given us directions in His Word for how we are to deal with the world in which we live. Orderliness is a quality of God. Disorderliness results from our fallen, sinful world. When we spiritually nurture others, we help to bring God's order into their lives.

His **WORD:** Genesis 1:24–31

KNOWING *His* **HEART**

1. According to verses 24 and 25, what type of order did God create in the world?

2. How does man's dominion over creation reflect God's image?

3. What evidence do you see in the natural world that the mandate to have dominion still applies?

4. How does society's emphasis on careers counter the command to be fruitful (verse 28)?

KNOWING *My* HEART

1. How does the principle of being fruitful apply to your responsibility to spiritually nurture others?

2. How did the curse in Genesis 3:17–19 affect our work in ruling over nature? How does it affect you?

3. How does the fact that sin creates disorder affect your helping others to grow spiritually?

4. According to Job 32:8, what is your foundation for nurturing?

My HEART IN *His* HANDS

"The belief in a God all-powerful, wise, and good is so essential to the moral order of the world and to the happiness of man."

—JAMES MADISON

LESSON 2

To Protect

In the exodus from Egypt, the pillar of cloud and fire was essential to the Hebrews' success. That pillar was the presence of God as their Protector. Until the Israelites made it through the desert and into the Promised Land, the pillar guided and protected them. In Exodus 14, the pillar separated them from Pharaoh's army, which was descending upon them. As Christians, we are the body of Christ on earth. When we let God work through us to nurture others, we can act as their "pillar of fire" to help protect them from their spiritual enemies. Sometimes our encouragement and help may be all that stands between them and the sins that may cripple their spirits.

His WORD: Exodus 14:5–20

KNOWING *His* HEART

1. Describe the strength of the enemy pursuing the Israelites (Exodus 14:5–9).

2. In contrast to the strength of the Egyptians, describe the weakness of the Israelites (see Exodus 12:37,38).

3. What was one important reason God protected the Israelites (Exodus 14:18)?

4. How might the people's emotions have changed after seeing the pillar of cloud move (Exodus 14:10,19,20)?

KNOWING *My* HEART

1. Do you have any fears about helping others to grow spiritually?

2. What can we expect God to do for us and those we nurture? (See 2 Chronicles 16:9.)

3. How can you represent a pillar of fire against spiritual enemies to someone you are nurturing?

4. How can you teach her to use God's armor as listed in Ephesians 6:10–18?

My HEART IN *His* HANDS

"God has something only you can do."
—LEWIS TIMBERLAKE

LESSON 3

To Express Love

In the Bible, God expresses His love for us openly and often. One of the most beloved Bible verses is John 3:16: "God so loved the world that He gave..." True love is expressed through words as well as actions. As parents, we know how important it is to both tell and show our children how much we love them. The individuals we disciple need to know that God loves them and that we love them. As we nurture others, we can show them the depths of God's love both through His Word and by what He has done for us. Jesus showed His disciples how much He loved them by serving them (John 13:1). We can follow His example by loving our friends in the same way.

His WORD: John 16:27,28

KNOWING *His* HEART

1. What are the similarities between John 16:27,28 and John 3:16?

2. What assurances of His love does God reveal in Romans 5:8,9?

3. Why do you think the Bible repeatedly states how much God loves us?

4. What is the depth of love that we should show to others (John 15:13)?

KNOWING *My* HEART

1. How important is it to you to have people express their love for you?

2. Why are both words and actions necessary to show love?

3. Name ways you can verbally express love to those you are spiritually nurturing.

4. How can you show love through actions in your nurturing opportunities?

My HEART IN *His* HANDS

"The strongest evidence of love is sacrifice."
—CAROLINE FRY

LESSON 4

To Motivate

Dr. Henrietta Mears, who was the Christian education director at my church in Hollywood, led me to Christ. She then took me under her wing and explained what God had done for me, how I could please Him, and how He wanted to change my life. She was thrilled to teach me all she knew about God. She helped me through tough times and prayed for me. Even today, years after she has gone to be with the Lord, her love and example motivate me to teach others and help them grow. I pass on to them what Miss Mears taught me. My desire is to motivate others to love God as she motivated me. In turn, I urge you to invest your life in someone you can train to serve Christ.

His WORD: Acts 11:19–26

KNOWING *His* HEART

1. What kinds of discouragement do you think the believers in Antioch might have faced?

2. What did Barnabas encourage the Antioch believers to do?

3. Why do you think Barnabas brought Saul to Antioch?

4. Barnabas's name means "son of encouragement." How does this quality relate to motivating others in the Lord?

KNOWING *My* HEART

1. When someone motivated you spiritually, what part did encouragement play?

2. How can you use that experience to help you nurture others?

3. When motivating other to grow spiritually, how can you balance encouragement with correction? (See Ephesians 4:15.)

4. Who does God want you to motivate to serve Him? How can you motivate this person?

My HEART IN *His* HANDS

"This process of passing our faith along to others and helping them grow toward maturity serves to increase our own desire and motivation to grow."
—DARREL HEIDE

LESSON 5

Through Example

My mother-in-law set an example for Bill that has lasted throughout his lifetime. One of the most important principles she lived before him was the necessity of a personal relationship with God through Bible reading and prayer. It was vital for him to actually see her consistently doing these things. In turn, Bill and I have tried to implant these same spiritual principles into the lives of our sons as well as other believers. For example, the young Campus Crusade for Christ staff women who serve with me, my sisters in Christ, are people in whom I can have an influence for our Lord. My desire is to leave spiritual generations behind me in every place I serve.

His **WORD:** 2 Timothy 2:1–7

KNOWING *His* HEART

1. According to 2 Timothy 2:2, how does discipleship become an ongoing process?

2. According to verse 1, what is needed to disciple others?

3. What is required to stay focused on the task (verses 3,4)?

4. How does Paul compare Christians to an athlete and a farmer?

KNOWING *My* HEART

1. What can you learn from Jesus' example about discipling in times of hardship?

2. What should you do if the person you are nurturing fails you in some area? (Think of Jesus and Peter.)

3. What tends to take your attention away from your nurturing focus?

4. Which illustration (athlete or farmer) is more helpful to you right now and why?

My HEART IN *His* HANDS

"No man is poor who has had a godly mother."
—ABRAHAM LINCOLN

PART 2

A Supernatural Response

If you travel through the gorgeous Central Valley in California, you will see acres and acres of fields. This agricultural area produces much of our nation's vegetables and fruits. The long growing season enables farmers to plant a huge variety of crops. Irrigation pumps shoot water over the thirsty plants. Even when the surrounding landscape is brown and barren, the fields will be vibrant green.

At any one time, you will see crops in all stages of growth. There will be bare, plowed fields, the rich earth lined with straight furrows waiting to be planted. Alongside the dark earth will be tender green shoots of vegetables just emerging from the soil. You will also notice acres of flowering strawberry mounds, huge-leafed cabbages, grapevines staked in rows, and fields of flowers. And periodically you will see a field dotted with harvesters picking the ripe fruit.

Occasionally, however, you will notice a field that has not been tilled or nurtured, filled with a ragged crop of weeds. What a contrast to the tended acres! One is in disorder; the other is in order. The first is fruitless; the other is fruitful.

We may also see this contrast in our own lives. When we nurture and care for our own spirit, mind, emotions, and body, we reap order and well-being. When we neglect our spiritual and physical fitness, we are unable to manage ourselves effectively.

The foundation for all of our well-being is spiritual health. Living by eternal principles in the power of the Holy Spirit undergirds our mental, emotional, and physical health. Even if we are ill or in the midst of an emotional crisis, our spiritual health will determine how well we handle difficulties in other areas. At the same time, as we nurture our spirits in the Lord, we will be more aware of what we need to do to build up our bodies, minds, and emotions in the Lord.

A productive field requires great effort, as any farmer can attest. Our spiritual health likewise demands our continual attention. Surely, we would chuckle at this way of thinking: "Last month, I planted weed seeds, but I expect roses to come up!" As ridiculous as that sounds, we are all guilty of following a similar pattern in nurturing our spirits. We think, "It's okay if I allow this one area of sin to grow in me. It won't affect me that much. My life will still produce just as much spiritual fruit."

The laws of the spiritual realm are no less binding than those of the natural realm. Nurturing our entire well-being takes a supernatural response. We must nurture each area in the power of the Holy Spirit, committing ourselves to obeying God's spiritual laws. In the following lessons, we will learn how we can fulfill our mandate from God to nurture by feeding our spirits, minds, emotions, and bodies.

LESSON 6

Nurturing the Spirit

A Sunday school class was discussing why some adult believers are sweet while others are cantankerous. The members concluded that the habits that a person practices in childhood yield "fruit" later in life. We can not only plant bad behavior, we can also "nurture" it, making it grow. When we ignore its presence, the sprout of sin that is easy to pull out soon becomes rooted in our spirit. It may seem cute when a child stomps her foot and says, "No!" but it is hideous when an adult flies into a rage. What are you doing to nurture godliness in your spirit? Ask God to help you produce spiritual fruit in your life.

His WORD: Galatians 6:7,8

KNOWING *His* HEART

1. What do you think Paul means when he writes, "Do not be deceived"?

2. How does Proverbs 22:8,9 explain the principle of sowing and reaping?

3. What does God promise when we plant faith in our lives (1 John 5:4)?

4. What will we eventually reap if we plant faith (2 Timothy 4:7,8)?

KNOWING *My* HEART

1. In what areas in your life do you lack faith in God's power and wisdom?

2. What spiritual "weeds" might you reap due to a lack of faith?

3. Describe a time when your faith produced supernatural results.

4. How can you use your faith to nurture the areas where you lack faith?

My HEART IN *His* HANDS

"God never goes back on the man who stakes his all on Him."

—WILLIAM BARCLAY

LESSON 7

Nurturing the Mind

The slogan "A mind is a terrible thing to waste" refers to a failure to educate young men and women, which is a tragedy. But an even greater calamity is when a mind is allowed to become a spiritual wasteland. As believers, we have been given the mind of Christ, but it is our responsibility, through the power of the Holy Spirit, to nurture our minds in all godliness. As we nurture our spirits in Christ, we can also build up our minds to be pure. This purity can be likened to the clean, fresh water we use in replenishing our gardens. Pollutants in our minds will prevent any fruit from developing, but pure minds will result in abundant, fruitful lives.

His **WORD:** Romans 8:5–9; 1 Corinthians 2:16

KNOWING *His* HEART

1. What are the two mindsets described in Romans 8:5–9 and their results?

2. How do these mindsets relate to purity of thought (Titus 1:15)?

3. What should our minds dwell on (Philippians 4:8,9)?

4. Describe what it means to "have the mind of Christ" (1 Corinthians 2:16).

KNOWING *My* HEART

1. What impurities of the mind are the most prevalent temptations in our society?

2. How do minds set on these impurities lead to unhealthy living or even death?

3. How can you nurture the mind of Christ in your life?

4. What difference will spiritually nurturing your mind have on your future?

My HEART IN *His* HANDS

"God guides through your heightened moral intelligence. 'Can you not of yourselves judge that which is right?' said Jesus. He expected us to think our way to right Christian conclusions."

—E. STANLEY JONES

LESS⊖N 8

Nurturing Our Emotions

Although women have a reputation for being overly emotional, I consider having a sensitive spirit to be a gift from God —as long as we use it properly. Emotions are the doorway to our hearts and allow us to empathize with others. But emotions become a problem when they control us rather than us controlling them. When we allow our feelings to take us on an emotional roller-coaster ride, we lose touch with God's plans for our lives. Nurturing our sensitive side means valuing our feelings of love, sadness, joy, and pain. Yet above all these feelings, God calls us to be steadfast in Him. Nurturing our emotions means submitting them to the control of the Holy Spirit.

His **WORD:** Philippians 1:27—2:4

KNOWING *His* HEART

1. What does this passage say about our conduct?

2. Why is it a privilege to suffer for our faith even though it doesn't feel good?

3. According to Philippians 2:14–16, what conduct should we avoid?

4. What emotional response should we always have regardless of circumstances (verses 17,18)?

KNOWING *My* HEART

1. In what circumstances in your life do you have uncontrolled emotions?

2. How does an attitude of joy nurture our emotional being?

3. How does rejoicing with others build us up?

4. What emotions tend to rob you of joy?

My HEART IN *His* HANDS

"The surest mark of a Christian is not faith, or even love, but joy."
—SAM SHOEMAKER

Nurturing Our Body

We are bombarded with advertisements for products that help our bodies: diet pills, exercise machines, health foods, vitamins. Although these are good for our health, one way to healthy living that the world rarely mentions is avoiding sin. Sin can devastate us physically. Consider alcoholism, AIDS, drug abuse, venereal disease. Any sin will wreak havoc on our bodies. In 1 Corinthians 6:19,20, Paul reminds us that our bodies are temples of God. What we do with our bodies deeply affects our spiritual, mental, and emotional growth. Nurturing our physical self leads to spiritual health. As we honor God with our bodies, we can encourage others to do the same.

His **WORD:** Romans 7:21—8:4

KNOWING *His* HEART

1. What does it mean to honor God with your body (1 Corinthians 6:19,20)?

2. Describe the raging battle Paul mentions in Romans 7:21–24.

3. What is the solution to victory in this battle (Romans 7:25—8:4)?

4. How does our mind help us nurture our bodies (Romans 8:5,6)?

KNOWING *My* HEART

1. How are you honoring God with your body?

2. In which areas is a battle raging between using your body for sin and for righteousness?

3. How could you set your mind on the Spirit in these areas?

4. In what specific ways can you encourage someone to honor God with her body?

My HEART IN *His* HANDS

"As we go up the scale of spiritual excellence, temptation follows us all the way, becoming more refined as our lives are more refined, more subtle as our spiritual sensitiveness is keener."

—A. VICTOR MURRAY

The Power of Emotions

In our society, emotions have become the benchmark for decisions. "If it feels good, do it." "I can't help the way I feel." Many times people use this reasoning to excuse sinful behavior and avoid guilt. But as Christians, we know that every sin is wrong, no matter where the temptation comes from or how powerful it is. And the freedom we experience when we use our emotions for doing what's right is incredible. Jochebed and her compatriots must have known tremendous fear living under the rule of Pharaoh. Yet through it all, God produced greatness. What a powerful story of how God helps us do what's right in the midst of our crippling emotions!

His **WORD:** Exodus 1:1–22

KNOWING *His* HEART

1. Why did Pharaoh command that all Hebrew male newborns be killed?

2. How did some Hebrew women defy the Pharaoh's edict?

3. What was the result of the faithfulness of these women (1:20, 21)?

4. What was Pharaoh's reaction to God's blessing?

KNOWING *My* HEART

1. How might Jochebed have felt during her pregnancy as all this terror was going on?

2. How might the example of the midwives have helped her?

3. What societal influences worry you as you raise your children (or help other children)?

4. How can the Jewish nation's example give you confidence?

My HEART IN *His* HANDS

"The woman who creates and sustains a home, and under whose hands children grow up to be strong and pure men and women, is a creator second only to God."

—HELEN HUNT JACKSON

PART 3

A Developed Gift

Some years ago, Janelle become a Christian and began attending a church for the first time. Although her husband was not a believer and didn't attend with her, she joined a young couples' Sunday school class. Debbie noticed Janelle, sat beside her, and introduced herself. As they talked, Janelle warmed up to Debbie's attention.

A few days later, Debbie invited Janelle to her home for lunch. Janelle eagerly accepted. As the two talked, Janelle began crying. "This is the first time I've ever been inside another Christian's home," she admitted. "I didn't know how wonderful it would feel to talk about the Lord with a friend."

Debbie was shocked at Janelle's words. She had always taken

for granted the close fellowship of her Christian family and friends. She couldn't imagine what it would be like to be unable to share her innermost joys with another person.

That afternoon began a friendship that has lasted for more than twenty years. The two immediately began meeting for a Bible study, and Debbie helped her new friend discover her role as a godly mother and wife. When Debbie moved out of state two years later, the two women stayed in contact, encouraging each other. Recently, when Janelle's husband unexpectedly died of a heart attack, she called Debbie, and the two spent time together crying and praying.

Nurturing other believers is an intentional ministry given to us by our loving God. He knows that building each other up in the faith helps both the person who nurtures and the one who receives the nurturing. And many times, we will find that circumstances may reverse and we will have the privilege of receiving from the person we nurtured.

The process of spiritual nurturing involves four steps: 1) Assess the person's need. 2) Pray fervently. 3) Be available to help. 4) Seek God's counsel.

We cannot help those to whom we minister unless we know what they need. Sometimes their most important need is not obvious. Underneath an apparent need is a deeper spiritual yearning. Once we know the need, we must take it to the Lord in prayer. Only He can truly meet the desires of a person's heart.

Planning how to meet a need requires that we be available to be used by God in that process. As we nurture her, we must seek God's wisdom for each step.

Practicing the process of nurturing enables us to develop skills in helping others. The Lord builds in us compassion, wisdom, and strength to serve others. It is a learning experience that brings us joy and satisfaction in every area of our lives.

Assess the Need

When the home health nurse made her initial visit to an elderly orthopedic patient, she made sure he understood the doctor's instructions he was given at the hospital. She examined the home to ensure he could safely use the bathroom, get into bed, and move around the house. She set up a schedule so that he would not become confused about his medications, and scheduled visits with a home therapist. The nurse made sure that all the patient's health needs were addressed. That's what we do for others to whom we minister. We assess what they need by getting to know where they are spiritually and emotionally, and how we can best help them to grow. As we assess needs, God gives us greater spiritual sensitivity about our nurturing role.

His WORD: 1 Thessalonians 2:7–12

KNOWING *His* HEART

1. What depth of care did Paul give to those he nurtured (verses 7–9)?

2. What qualities did he exhibit in his work among them (verse 10)?

3. What actions did he take in his nurturing role (verses 11,12)?

4. What instruction does Paul give in 2 Timothy 2:24?

KNOWING *My* HEART

1. What did Paul mean by saying that they shared "not only the gospel of God but our lives as well"?

2. What parenting qualities could you practice in nurturing?

3. How does Paul inspire you to keep working with those struggling through difficult circumstances?

4. How can Paul's instruction to avoid quarreling and resentment help you in a current nurturing situation?

My HEART IN *His* HANDS

"Love has hands to help others. It has feet to hasten to the poor and needy. It has eyes to see misery and want. It has ears to hear the sighs and sorrows of men. This is what love looks like."

—St. Augustine

Pray Fervently

Prayer is the tool that gives our nurturing eternal significance. Without prayer, we cannot achieve eternal success. Christians in the early church faced incredible pressures that could have made them retreat into their homes in fear. Yet these believers reached out into their community, helping those of the faith and many who did not believe. As a result, within a few decades, they had changed their world for Christ. These faithful saints relied on prayer to defeat spiritual enemies and to help them build each other up in the faith. Just like them, we desperately need the power that prayer gives. We may not face the physical dangers that the first-century believers encountered, but our enemy is the same. Prayer still defeats that enemy and gives us the strength and wisdom to nurture others.

His **WORD:** Colossians 4:12,13

KNOWING *His* **HEART**

1. How did Epaphras show his concern for those he nurtured?

2. What was the subject of his prayers?

3. What was Paul's opinion of Epaphras (verse 13)?

4. What does Paul say about the character of Epaphras in Colossians 1:7,8?

KNOWING *My* HEART

1. How would you describe your prayer life for the people you are nurturing?

2. How does your ministry to others differ when you fail to pray and when you "wrestle" in prayer?

3. How can you apply Colossians 3:16,17 to your ministry?

4. What part should thankfulness play in your prayers?

My HEART IN *His* HANDS

"*God does nothing but in answer to prayer.*"
—JOHN WESLEY

LESSON 13

Be Available

If you've planted tomato seedlings in the spring, you know the thrill of harvesting your own crop. You won't see much growth right after placing the plant in the soil, but it is sending out roots, establishing itself in its environment. Then when it begins to grow, you can almost see it gaining height each day. If left untended, the branches will become so heavy that they will fall to the ground. A gardener places a tomato cage around the plant to help support the branches as they bear fruit. As the tomatoes become meatier, the tomato cage prevents the fruit from touching the ground and rotting. That's the principle of being available. As the tomato cage supports the plant while the branches mature, so should we be available to our friends and loved ones to support them as they grow in their faith.

His WORD: Acts 9:10–19

KNOWING His HEART

1. How did Ananias respond when God called him to help Paul (Saul)?

2. What was the result of Ananias's obedience (verses 17,18)?

3. What do you think happened in Damascus over the next few days (verse 19)?

4. What would Ananias have missed if he had not been available to God's call?

KNOWING *My* HEART

1. In what ways has God called you to be available for His work?

2. What happened during a time when you closed your heart to God's call?

3. What does it means to be available to a person you are nurturing?

4. What part do your prayers play in being available?

My HEART IN *His* HANDS

"Man's greatest sin is not hatred, but indifference to one's brothers."
— MOTHER TERESA

LESSON 14

Seek God's Counsel

As we nurture, we sometimes feel inadequate for the job. How can we handle the problems that our friends face? Where can we find solutions? Jesse found herself worrying about some of the marital problems faced by her friend Amber. The difficulties seemed more than Jesse could handle as a spiritual advisor, so she enlisted the aid of a more experienced counselor. This woman knew the Bible well and had practical experience applying it in family crises. The three of them addressed Amber's problem based on the wisdom in God's Word. We can encourage those we mentor to seek God's counsel for their situations by praying and studying the Scriptures.

His WORD: Isaiah 46:9–11

KNOWING *His* HEART

1. Why is it important to seek God's counsel (Isaiah 46:9–11)?

2. According to Psalm 119:24–28, what is one way of seeking God's counsel and the result?

3. What is another way of seeking God's counsel (Jeremiah 33:3)?

4. What is a result of receiving godly counsel from others (Proverbs 12:15; 15:22)?

KNOWING *My* HEART

1. Describe a time when you sought counsel in God's Word for a friend in a difficult situation.

2. How did prayer help you both resolve the problem?

3. What is the danger in nurturing someone without receiving the counsel of other godly believers?

4. How can you help your disciple seek God's counsel as you do?

My HEART IN *His* HANDS

"The strength of a man consists in finding out the way in which God is going, and going that way too."

—HENRY WARD BEECHER

Be Faithful

Mary Lee Bright didn't have the technological advantages in nurturing her household that many of us have today. Her daily responsibilities took more of her time. She also didn't have the resources of dynamic ministries and the Christian books that we have. But those things weren't necessary for her to fulfill her role. She did what was necessary—study her Bible, pray, and be faithful in church attendance. She knew that the woman of God fulfills her role by becoming more like Christ and encouraging these qualities in those she loved. She most likely struggled with occasional times of discouragement, setbacks, and difficulties in modeling her walk with the Lord, yet she was faithful to the day she died. And the people who knew her best recognized and acknowledged her service for them.

His **WORD:** Hebrews 3:1–6

KNOWING *His* **HEART**

1. In this passage, how is Jesus similar to Moses?

2. How is Jesus superior to Moses (verses 3–6)?

3. How is our relationship with Christ pictured in verse 6?

4. How is Moses' example a reflection of his parents' nurturing (Hebrews 11:23)?

KNOWING *My* HEART

1. What part does faithfulness play in spiritual nurturing?

2. What have you learned about Mary Lee Bright's life that can help you be faithful?

3. As children of God, what can we learn from our heavenly Father to help us nurture others?

4. Identify one person God has laid on your heart whom you can faithfully nurture.

My HEART IN *His* HANDS

"*If I am faithful to the duties of the present, God will provide for the future.*"
—GREGORY T. BEDELL

PART 4

The Objects of My Affection

What do you most value in your house? I have many items that I have collected through the years. I treasure them because they remind me of someone I love or of events that made a difference in people's lives.

Women collect many things. Some love antique dishes, with their delicate patterns and pleasing colors, and display their favorites in china hutches. Other women consider their home to be their treasure, and they take great care to decorate it with cherished furnishings. As you walk into their homes, you can see the attention they have given to every detail. When we work hard to collect certain items, we cherish them and make sure they are maintained in a certain way.

These tangible treasures are good and appropriate—as long as they remain in their rightful place in our lives. But when they become more important than the people we love, they assume a larger influence over us than our Lord desires. An example is a woman who is so careful about her home that her family cannot live comfortably. The children cannot play with their toys because they might damage or break them. No one can roughhouse in the family room because something might get broken.

In God's eyes, our things are to be used for nurturing the loved ones and friends in our lives. When viewed from an eternal perspective, any object we own is expendable. On the other hand, people have immortal souls. Therefore, the objects of our affection should be those whom God has placed in our nurturing circle: our neighbors, our family, our friends. God expects us to be role models of His love and grace to them.

Romans 12:10 says, "Be devoted to one another in brotherly love. Honor one another above yourselves." If we honor others above ourselves, we will do what's best for them rather than considering our own desires. Mothers of preschoolers naturally practice this principle. I have four beautiful grandchildren, but they take time and energy to raise. I have seen times when my two daughters-in-love were exhausted from caring for their little ones, but they kept on hugging squirming bodies, reading books, cooking, and cleaning until they fell into bed at night. I remember doing the same with my two sons. I've seen incredibly busy women find time to whip up a dinner for an ill neighbor. I've talked to friends who put aside activities they loved so that they could minister to someone in the midst of a crisis.

These lessons will help encourage you to nurture the people God has placed in your life. Giving these dear ones priority will bring you immense joy and satisfaction.

LESSON 16

Being a Role Model

The Bible gives us a great number of role models that we can follow in our spiritual nurturing responsibilities. Of course, the first and foremost role model is Jesus Christ. We are given many stories of how He handled Himself with different kinds of people: His disciples, women, children, the ill, those caught in sin, those opposed to His ministry. Likewise, the apostle Paul demonstrated how we should treat fellow believers and how we should endure through difficult situations. He loved those in the churches scattered around the Middle East. He encouraged and taught the believers, either in person or by letter. We, too, can build up those we love. Today's passage gives us clear instructions on how to spiritually nurture others.

His WORD: Colossians 2:1–5

KNOWING His HEART

1. List ways you can nurture others according to Paul's example.

2. How did Paul try to protect those he nurtured (verse 4)?

3. According to 2 Timothy 2:15, what goal should we have as we nurture others?

4. In 2 Timothy 2:14,16, what does a workman avoid when helping others?

KNOWING *My* HEART

1. In what ways do you engage in quarreling or "godless chatter"?

2. How can looking to God help you change how you talk with those you nurture?

3. In what ways are you studying God's Word to make yourself a better role model as a nurturer and teacher?

4. What part does humility play in being a role model?

My HEART IN *His* HANDS

"Nurturing one another is what it's all about, and this generation has a long way to go before we love too much."

—MARIANNE WILLIAMSON

Loving My Neighbor

The Schulers were involved in an accident in which their daughter, Vanessa, was thrown from the vehicle and landed on her head. She was in a coma for three days before she died. Mark and Debbie learned of their tragedy through a neighbor. They'd never met Tom and Jan Schuler, but they could not get them off their minds. Mark found the Schulers' telephone number and the two couples met. A deep and lasting friendship was formed, and Tom eventually accepted Christ as his Savior. This story illustrates Jesus' parable of the Good Samaritan. In it He teaches us that hurting people are our neighbors, and it is our responsibility to nurture those whom God places in our path.

His WORD: Luke 10:25–37

KNOWING His HEART

1. How does Mark 12:31, part of the Great Commandment, help explain this parable?

2. What shows that the Samaritan was not acting out of guilt or a sense of duty?

3. What does it mean to "do likewise"?

4. How does Matthew 5:7 relate to what Jesus was teaching in the parable?

KNOWING *My* HEART

1. Which ministries in your church help fulfill Christ's command to be a neighbor?

2. How are you participating in these ministries?

3. Do you know your neighbors? How can you get to know them better?

4. How does desiring to be a role model for Christ help you love your neighbor as much as yourself?

My HEART IN *His* HANDS

"Let me be a little meeker / With the brother that is weaker,
Let me think more of my neighbor / And a little less of me."

—EDGAR A. GUEST

Training Up My Children

Today, children face more temptations, negative influences, and pressures than ever before: Internet pornography, violent video games, sexually oriented music and movies, profanity on television, and the teaching of anti-biblical theories and morals. As parents and grandparents, our job is immense, but God gives us the needed strength and wisdom. However, we can only disciple others as far as we have grown spiritually ourselves. If we aren't willing to press on with our own spiritual race, our children may not get off the starting block in theirs. This is where we perform our most essential work as godly role models by protecting, loving, and motivating.

His WORD: Deuteronomy 4:9

KNOWING *His* HEART

1. According to Deuteronomy 4:9, what is the process of family discipleship?

2. How was this pattern displayed in 2 Timothy 1:5?

3. What does Deuteronomy 6:6–9 tell us about how to implement this discipleship process?

4. What is the commandment given to us in 2 Corinthians 12:14 about physical care?

KNOWING *My* HEART

1. How are you applying the instruction in Proverbs 22:6?

2. How are you building up your own spiritual health so you can edify others?

3. Which areas of your discipleship to your (grand)children do you need to strengthen?

4. How can you deepen your prayer life with and for your (grand)children?

My HEART IN *His* HANDS

"Children need models rather than critics."

—JOSEPH JOUBERT

Building Up My Friends

W hile in England, Carolyn's husband was diagnosed with a brain tumor that required him to be hospitalized for six months. There Carolyn met Sophie, a tiny woman from Ghana who served tea at the hospital. Carolyn asked her if she knew Jesus, but the answer became obvious—yes! Carolyn, an experienced discipler, suddenly found herself in the "student" role. Sophie taught her so much about nurturing in those difficult days. Carolyn had always seen herself as the one who could step into someone's life and help—be the wise one, the healer, the teacher. But Sophie was more like Jesus, bringing hope, love, and grace. When we walk with God, we can be used by Him in another person's life—no matter what our position.

His **WORD:** Philippians 1:3–11

KNOWING *His* HEART

1. What are Paul's feelings for the Philippian believers?

2. How long will God work with believers to help them grow in Christ (verse 6)?

3. What specific things does Paul desire to build into the lives of the Philippians (verses 9–11)?

4. What is the goal of a discipleship relationship (verse 11)?

KNOWING *My* HEART

1. Seeing Paul's example, what principles can you apply to your work of nurturing others?

2. What part has affection for others played in your ministry to them?

3. How are you building spiritual knowledge and depth of insight in the lives of those you nurture?

4. What fruits of righteousness do you want to see blossom in the lives of your friends?

My HEART IN *His* HANDS

"Our task as laymen is to live out our personal communion with Christ with such intensity as to make it contagious."

—PAUL TOURNIER

God's Power

Jochebed is an example of a woman who gave her all for her children. She was inventive, focused, and godly. I'm sure there were many other mothers in her situation who were paralyzed by fear and sorrow. And I'm sure Jochebed had her misgivings as she shaped the little basket that would hold one of her dearest treasures. She must have also built great character in her daughter, Miriam, for her to behave so boldly. How amazed she must have been when Miriam came running to bring her to Pharaoh's daughter to nurse the baby! How the entire family must have praised God that night as she held her newborn again in her own home surrounded by those she loved!

His WORD: Exodus 2:1–10

KNOWING His HEART

1. What characteristics of Jochebed can you see in Miriam?

2. What shows God was working behind the scenes for Jochebed?

3. How did God provide nurturing, both secular and religious, to prepare Moses for his future leadership role?

4. How does this story show that God's power is displayed in our weakness (2 Corinthians 12:9)?

KNOWING *My* HEART

1. How does this story show the power of nurturing within the family?

2. What does this story say about the importance of modeling your faith before others?

3. How can the story of Moses encourage those you disciple to take leadership roles in the body of Christ?

4. What new steps are you willing to take in nurturing now that you have seen the power of God to help you disciple others?

My HEART IN *His* HANDS

"Success is living in such a way that you are using what God has given you—your intellect, abilities, and energy—to reach the purpose He intends for your life."

—KATHI HUDSON

Discussion Guide

The following pages contain information to help you use the Bible studies in this Guide. If you are using the *Nurturing Heart* lessons as a group study, the answers to the questions will help your facilitator guide the discussion. If you are studying the lessons on your own, refer to the answers after you have finished the lesson.

Answers are given for the first section of questions, called "Knowing HIS Heart." These questions are objective searches through the lesson's Bible passage. The second section, "Knowing MY Heart," are personal application questions and are written to help you use the Bible truths in your everyday life. Therefore, these questions will pertain to your individual situations.

If you are leading a group, work through the first section more thoroughly. Then allow volunteers to give answers to the second section of questions. Some answers may be so personal that your group members will not want to express them aloud. Be sensitive to your group members' feelings in this area.

The Lord bless you are you apply the steps to wisdom in your life!

Part 1: The Nurturing Instinct

LESSON 1: BY GOD'S DESIGN

1. He made each type of creature according to kinds.

2. Just as God is sovereign over all creation, He has delegated to us the responsibility to rule over what He has created. We are

to reflect God's caring nature for us as we care for other creatures.

3. Animals are afraid of humans; we can subdue even the fiercest animals. People are able to control much of nature in all parts of the world.

4. People don't value having and raising children as much now. People are more interested in their own advancement than in nurturing a family. Women are having fewer children and may even abort children when they interfere with their career plans.

LESSON 2: TO PROTECT

1. Pharaoh sent six hundred of the best chariots plus all the other chariots in Egypt, along with horses, horsemen, and troops.

2. The Israelites were on foot, and included women, children, and the elderly. They also brought all their livestock and household goods, so they were very vulnerable to attack. Because the men had been slaves, not soldiers, they didn't know how to wage war.

3. God wanted Pharaoh and all the Egyptians to give God glory.

4. They initially were terrified, but when they saw God's protection, they surely were heartened and encouraged that God was going to preserve them.

LESSON 3: TO EXPRESS LOVE

1. Both tell us that the Son of God came into the world because of God's love for us. We must believe in Him to have eternal life.

2. God loved us even though we were sinners. He loves us so much that He will save us from His wrath.

3. We find it difficult to comprehend His unconditional love for us. Being reminded of His love helps us remain grateful to Him.

4. We should lay down our lives for others.

LESSON 4: TO MOTIVATE

1. They had been scattered by persecution so they may have felt disoriented and afraid. They were new believers and under a lot of social pressure because of their new faith. They didn't know much about how to live the Christian life.

2. He encouraged them to stay true to the Lord.

3. He may have needed help teaching the new believers in Antioch. Perhaps he was helping Paul learn how to disciple Christians. Paul may have been an encouragement to Barnabas.

4. Discipling involves motivating others to apply biblical teaching. Encouragement is an essential part of the process. If people become discouraged, they will not be motivated to go on.

LESSON 5: THROUGH EXAMPLE

1. As we disciple one believer, that person is to teach others who in turn will be able to teach others.

2. We must be strong in the grace that is in Jesus.

3. We must endure hardship, not get caught up in worldly concerns, and desire to please our Commander, Jesus.

4. We will receive a reward if we follow the rules, like the athlete, and if we work hard, like the farmer.

Part 2: A Supernatural Response

LESSON 6: NURTURING THE SPIRIT

1. We should never fall for the argument that we can commit sin and not reap the negative consequences. God sees all of our activities and will hold us accountable.

2. Sowing wickedness reaps trouble and destruction. Sowing generosity will reap blessings.

3. We will overcome the world.

4. We will receive a crown of righteousness from Jesus.

LESSON 7: NURTURING THE MIND

1. A mind set on sinful desires results in death. A mind set on the Spirit results in life.

2. The spiritual mindset dwells on pure thoughts. The sinful mindset is corrupted and dwells on what is impure.

3. Whatever is true, noble, right, pure, lovely, admirable, excellent, praiseworthy. Whatever we learn from Paul's example, we should put into practice.

4. To allow Christ's Holy Spirit to think through us. To follow Christ's example in attitude at all times.

LESSON 8: NURTURING OUR EMOTIONS

1. We are to always act worthy of the gospel, in unity contending for the faith and being unafraid.

2. We are suffering for the name of Christ. Just as Paul's struggles were an example to the Philippians, our suffering can encourage others who are suffering.

3. Complaining and arguing.

4. We should always be glad and rejoice.

LESSON 9: NURTURING OUR BODY

1. We are to consider our body as a temple of God, holy for His purposes, and not use it for impure activities that would dishonor God.

2. In his mind he delights in God's law and wants to do good, but his body tempts him to sin.

3. Christ's death for us sets us free; we are no longer slaves to our sinful nature but live according to the Spirit.

4. Setting our minds on what the Spirit desires leads to life and peace.

LESSON 10: THE POWER OF EMOTIONS

1. He was afraid that the Hebrew people would get too powerful and would cause him problems or throw off the yoke of slavery. He thought that by eliminating a generation of males, he could keep them subdued.

2. Rather than killing all the boy babies that they delivered, the midwives told Pharaoh that the Hebrew women gave birth before the midwives arrived.

3. God protected the midwives, gave them their own families, and increased the number of Hebrews in spite of the Pharaoh.

4. He gave an order to all Egyptians that every Hebrew baby boy be thrown into the river. He circumvented the midwives and made the situation even worse for a time.

Part 3: A Developed Gift

LESSON 11: ASSESS THE NEED

1. He treated them gently, like a mother caring for her children. He loved them and shared the gospel and his very life with them. He worked day and night not to be a burden to them.

2. He was holy, righteous, and blameless.

3. Like a father dealing with his children, he encouraged and comforted them and urged them to live holy lives.

4. When we nurture others, we shouldn't quarrel or be resentful, but instead act kindly as we teach.

LESSON 12: PRAY FERVENTLY

1. He was always wrestling in prayer for them.

2. That the believers would stand firm in God's will, grow spiritually, be confident in their faith.

3. He assured the Colossians that Epaphras was working hard for them and for others he served.

4. He was a dear fellow servant and a faithful minister of Christ.

LESSON 13: BE AVAILABLE

1. At first he was hesitant because of Paul's reputation as a persecutor of the Christians, but he obeyed God and went immediately to where Paul was staying.

2. Paul was healed of his blindness, was filled with the Holy Spirit, and was baptized.

3. As the disciples were teaching Paul about Jesus, people were

probably initially doubtful about his sincerity and then amazed at his transformation.

4. He would not have experienced the beginnings of Paul's ministry and would not have seen the miracles God performed at that time.

LESSON 14: SEEK GOD'S COUNSEL

1. Because God knows everything, from beginning to end, and He will ensure that His plans are carried out, we should consult Him first.

2. We seek God's counsel by reading and studying His Word. He will teach us His decrees, help us understand them, and strengthen us.

3. When we seek God regularly in prayer, He will instruct us.

4. Listening to advice will help us be wiser. Our plans will succeed.

LESSON 15: BE FAITHFUL

1. Jesus was faithful to the One who appointed Him, as was Moses. Moses was found worthy, as was Jesus. Moses was a faithful servant, as was Jesus.

2. Jesus is given greater honor because He is God; Moses was just a man. As the Creator, Jesus has greater honor than the created. In God's house, Moses was a faithful servant; Jesus is a faithful Son.

3. We are God's house (His dwelling place), while Christ is the Son who has charge over us.

4. They built into his life a love for God and a willingness to sacrifice all to do God's will. They did not live by fear, but by their faith.

Part 4: The Objects of My Affection

LESSON 16: BEING A ROLE MODEL

1. Encourage others; help them understand God and know the treasures that are found in Christ; be concerned about them even when you aren't with them.

2. He taught them the truths of Scripture so that they would not be deceived by arguments from others who were teaching against God's Word.

3. We should always do everything to be approved by God and to correctly handle God's Word.

4. Quarreling and using godless chatter.

LESSON 17: LOVING MY NEIGHBOR

1. The Samaritan was fulfilling the command to "love your neighbor as yourself" when he helped the man alongside the road. This is the kind of selfless concern that Jesus wants us to have for others.

2. He went above and beyond what was expected. He not only dressed the man's wounds, he also paid for his lodging, gave the innkeeper money to take care of the man, and promised to cover any additional expenses.

3. Jesus was commanding us to be self-sacrificing with hurting people, even people we don't know personally.

4. If we act like the Samaritan and show mercy to those we meet, God will show mercy to us in our situations.

LESSON 18: TRAINING UP MY CHILDREN

1. We are to remember and treasure in our hearts the things we have learned, and we are to pass them on to our children and grandchildren.

2. Grandmother Lois passed on her faith to mother Eunice who passed it on to her son, Timothy.

3. We are to model loving God with all our hearts and talk about how to serve God with our children at all times wherever we are.

4. We are to provide for our children's material needs.

LESSON 19: BUILDING UP MY FRIENDS

1. He thanks God for them, he joyfully prays for them, they are in his heart, he longs for them with the affection of Christ.

2. He will continue working in each believer until the job is completed at the day of Jesus Christ's second coming.

3. Love that grows in knowledge and depth of insight, spiritual discernment, the fruit of righteousness.

4. The glory and praise of God.

LESSON 20: GOD'S POWER

1. Like Jochebed, Miriam was willing to take risks to save the baby. Like Jochebed, Miriam was creative in suggesting that she could find a Hebrew woman to nurse the baby.

2. The child was discovered by Pharaoh's daughter, the one person who could save the baby's life. The mother not only was able to raise her new baby, but she was paid to do so, probably no small matter for a family raised in slavery.

3. God allowed Moses to receive training and education in Pharaoh's household, and also to be nurtured in the Jewish faith by his mother.

4. Jochebed had few resources to help her baby, but she did what she could, and God worked the situation out better than she could have even dreamed possible.

Beginning Your Journey of Joy

These four principles are essential in beginning a journey of joy.

One—*God loves you and created you to know Him personally.*

God's Love

"God so loved the world that He gave His one and only Son, that whoever believes in Him shall not perish but have eternal life" (John 3:16).

God's Plan

"Now this is eternal life: that they may know you, the only true God, and Jesus Christ, whom you have sent" (John 17:3).

What prevents us from knowing God personally?

Two—*People are sinful and separated from God, so we cannot know Him personally or experience His love.*

People are Sinful

"All have sinned and fall short of the glory of God" (Romans 3:23).

People were created to have fellowship with God; but, because of our own stubborn self-will, we chose to go our own independent way and fellowship with God was broken. This self-will, characterized by an attitude of active rebellion or passive indifference, is an evidence of what the Bible calls sin.

People are Separated

"The wages of sin is death" [spiritual separation from God] (Romans 6:23).

This diagram illustrates that God is holy and people are sinful. A great gulf separates the two. The arrows illustrate that people are continually trying to reach God and establish a personal relationship with Him through our own efforts, such as a good life, philosophy, or religion—but we inevitably fail.

The third principle explains the only way to bridge this gulf...

Three—*Jesus Christ is God's only provision for our sin. Through Him alone we can know God personally and experience His love.*

He Died In Our Place

"God demonstrates His own love toward us, in that while we were yet sinners, Christ died for us" (Romans 5:8).

He Rose from the Dead

"Christ died for our sins...He was buried...He was raised on the third day according to the Scriptures...He appeared to Peter, then to the twelve. After that He appeared to more than five hundred..." (1 Corinthians 15:3–6).

He Is the Only Way to God

"Jesus said to him, 'I am the way, and the truth, and the life; no one comes to the Father but through Me'" (John 14:6).

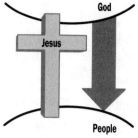

This diagram illustrates that God has bridged the gulf that separates us from Him by sending His Son, Jesus Christ, to die on the cross in our place to pay the penalty for our sins.

It is not enough just to know these three truths...

Four—We must individually receive Jesus Christ as Savior and Lord; then we can know God personally and experience His love.

We Must Receive Christ

"As many as received Him, to them He gave the right to become children of God, even to those who believe in His name" (John 1:12).

We Receive Christ Through Faith

"By grace you have been saved through faith; and that not of yourselves, it is the gift of God; not as a result of works that no one should boast" (Ephesians 2:8,9).

When We Receive Christ, We Experience a New Birth
(Read John 3:1–8.)

We Receive Christ By Personal Invitation

[Christ speaking] "Behold, I stand at the door and knock; if anyone hears My voice and opens the door, I will come in to him" (Revelation 3:20).

Receiving Christ involves turning to God from self (repentance) and trusting Christ to come into our lives to forgive us of our sins and to make us what He wants us to be. Just to agree intellectually that Jesus Christ is the Son of God and that He died on the cross for our sins is not enough. Nor is it enough to have an emotional experience. We receive Jesus Christ by faith, as an act of our will.

These two circles represent two kinds of lives:

Self-Directed Life
S – Self is on the throne
† – Christ is outside the
   life
● – Interests are directed
   by self, often resulting
   in discord and frustration

Christ-Directed Life
† – Christ is in the life
   and on the throne
S – Self is yielding to Christ
● – Interests are directed
   by Christ, resulting in har-
   mony with God's plan

Which circle best represents your life?
Which circle would you like to have represent your life?

The following explains how you can receive Christ:

You Can Receive Christ Right Now by Faith Through Prayer
(Prayer is talking with God)
God knows your heart and is not so concerned with your words as He is with the attitude of your heart. The following is a suggested prayer:

> *Lord Jesus, I want to know You personally. Thank You for dying on the cross for my sins. I open the door of my life and receive You as my Savior and Lord. Thank You for forgiving my sins and giving me eternal life. Take control of the throne of my life. Make me the kind of person You want me to be.*

Does this prayer express the desire of your heart?

If it does, I invite you to pray this prayer right now, and Christ will come into your life, as He promised.

How to Know That Christ Is in Your Life
Did you receive Christ into your life? According to His promise in Revelation 3:20, where is Christ right now in relation to you?

Christ said that He would come into your life. Would He mislead you? On what authority do you know that God has answered your prayer? (The trustworthiness of God Himself and His Word.)

The Bible Promises Eternal Life to All Who Receive Christ

"The witness is this, that God has given us eternal life, and this life is in His Son. He who has the Son has the life; he who does not have the Son of God does not have the life. These things I have written to you who believe in the name of the Son of God, in order that you may know that you have eternal life" (1 John 5:11–13).

Thank God often that Christ is in your life and that He will never leave you (Hebrews 13:5). You can know on the basis of His promise that Christ lives in you and that you have eternal life from the very moment you invite Him in. He will not deceive you.

An important reminder…

Feelings Can Be Unreliable

You might have expectations about how you should feel after placing your trust in Christ. While feelings are important, they are unreliable indicators of your sincerity or the trustworthiness of God's promise. Our feelings change easily, but God's Word and His character remain constant. This illustration shows the relationship among **fact** (God and His Word), **faith** (our trust in God and His Word), and our **feelings**.

Fact: The chair is strong enough to support you.

Faith: You believe this chair will support you, so you sit in it.

Feeling: You may or may not feel comfortable in this chair, but it continues to support you.

The promise of God's Word, the Bible—not our feelings—is our authority. The Christian lives by faith (trust) in the trustworthiness of God Himself and His Word.

Now That You Have Entered Into a Personal Relationship With Christ

The moment you received Christ by faith, as an act of your will, many things happened, including the following:

- Christ came into your life (Revelation 3:20; Colossians 1:27).
- Your sins were forgiven (Colossians 1:14).
- You became a child of God (John 1:12).
- You received eternal life (John 5:24).
- You began the great adventure for which God created you (John 10:10; 2 Corinthians 5:17; 1 Thessalonians 5:18).

Can you think of anything more wonderful that could happen to you than entering into a personal relationship with Jesus Christ? Would you like to thank God in prayer right now for what He has done for you? By thanking God, you demonstrate your faith.

To enjoy your new relationship with God...

Suggestions for Christian Growth

Spiritual growth results from trusting Jesus Christ. "The righteous man shall live by faith" (Galatians 3:11). A life of faith will enable you to trust God increasingly with every detail of your life, and to practice the following:

G   *Go* to God in prayer daily (John 15:7).

R   *Read* God's Word daily (Acts 17:11); begin with the Gospel of John.

O   *Obey* God moment by moment (John 14:21).

W   *Witness* for Christ by your life and words (Matthew 4:19; John 15:8).

T   *Trust* God for every detail of your life (1 Peter 5:7).

H   *Holy Spirit*—allow Him to control and empower your daily life and witness (Galatians 5:16,17; Acts 1:8; Ephesians 5:18).

Fellowship in a Good Church

God's Word admonishes us not to forsake "the assembling of ourselves together" (Hebrews 10:25). Several logs burn brightly together, but put one aside on the cold hearth and the fire goes out. So it is with your relationship with other Christians. If you do not belong to a church, do not wait to be invited. Take the initiative; call the pastor of a nearby church where Christ is honored and His Word is preached. Start this week, and make plans to attend regularly.

Resources

My Heart in His Hands: Renew a Steadfast Spirit Within Me.
Spring—renewal is everywhere; we are reminded to cry out to
God, "Renew a steadfast spirit within me." The first of four books
in Vonette Bright's devotional series, this book will give fresh
spiritual vision and hope to women of all ages. ISBN 1-56399-
161-6

My Heart in His Hands: Set Me Free Indeed. Summer—a
time of freedom. Are there bonds that keep you from God's
best? With this devotional, a few moments daily can help you
draw closer to the One who gives true freedom. This is the second of four in the devotional series. ISBN 1-56399-162-4

My Heart in His Hands: I Delight Greatly in My Lord. Do
you stop to appreciate the blessings God has given you? Spend
time delighting in God with book three in this devotional
series. ISBN 1-56399-163-2

My Heart in His Hands: Lead Me in the Way Everlasting. We
all need guidance, and God is the ultimate leader. These daily
moments with God will help you to rely on His leadership. The
final in the four-book devotional series. ISBN 1-56399-164-0

My Heart in His Hands: Bible Study Guides. Designed to
complement the four devotional books in this series, the Bible
Study Guides allow a woman to examine God's Word and gain
perspective on the issues that touch her life. Each study high-
lights a biblical character and includes an inspirational portrait

of a woman who served God. Available in 2002:
A Renewed Heart (1-56399-176-4)
A Nurturing Heart (1-56399-177-2)
A Woman's Heart (1-56399-178-0)
A Free Heart (1-56399-179-9)
A Wise Heart (1-56399-180-2)
A Caring Heart (1-56399-181-0)

The Joy of Hospitality: Fun Ideas for Evangelistic Entertaining. Co-written with Barbara Ball, this practical book tells how to share your faith through hosting barbecues, coffees, holiday parties, and other events in your home. ISBN 1-56399-057-1

The Joy of Hospitality Cookbook. Filled with uplifting scriptures and quotations, this cookbook contains hundreds of delicious recipes, hospitality tips, sample menus, and family traditions that are sure to make your entertaining a memorable and eternal success. Co-written with Barbara Ball. ISBN 1-56399-077-6

The Greatest Lesson I've Ever Learned. In this treasury of inspiring, real-life experiences, twenty-three prominent women of faith share their "greatest lessons." Does God have faith- and character-building lessons for you in their rich, heart-warming stories? ISBN 1-56399-085-7

Beginning Your Journey of Joy. This adaptation of the *Four Spiritual Laws* speaks in the language of today's women and offers a slightly feminine approach to sharing God's love with your neighbors, friends, and family members. ISBN 1-56399-093-8

These and other fine products from *NewLife* Publications are available from your favorite bookseller or by calling (800) 235-7255 (within U.S.) or (407) 826-2145, or by visiting www.newlifepubs.com.